BACKYARD BIRDS
WEST

A SEYMORE GULLS FIELD GUIDE
PHOTOS BY BRIAN E. SMALL

Scott & Nix, Inc.
NEW YORK

T0018432

PUBLISHED BY
SCOTT & NIX, INC.
150 W 28TH ST, STE 1900
NEW YORK, NY 10001
SCOTTANDNIX.COM

FIRST EDITION 2023

ISBN 978-1-935622-78-9

SCOTT & NIX, INC. BOOKS ARE DISTRIBUTED TO THE TRADE BY
INDEPENDENT PUBLISHERS GROUP (IPG)
814 NORTH FRANKLIN STREET
CHICAGO, IL 60610
800-888-4741
IPGBOOK.COM

THE PAPER OF THIS BOOK IS FSC CERTIFIED, WHICH ASSURES
IT WAS MADE FROM WELL MANAGED FORESTS AND OTHER
CONTROLLED SOURCES.

PRINTED IN CHINA THROUGH PORTER PRINT GROUP, BETHESDA, MARYLAND

BACKYARD BIRDS

WEST

GULF OF ALASKA

PACIFIC OCEAN

This books covers a
selection of common
species found in backyards
in the western continental
United States and Canada.

AK

YT

BC

AB

WA

MT

OR

ID

WY

NV

UT

CO

CA

AZ

NM

CONTENTS

I know it's crazy to write another bird book when there are already so many great guides out there. But, I'll do almost anything to get more people interested in looking at these wonderful little dinosaurs. And besides, I really wanted to "keep it simple" and "keep it fun." So, I present to you, *Backyard Birds West: A Seymore Gulls Bird Guide.* It's for those of us that love big pictures and just a little bit of text. A guide with the lowest barrier to entry possible. A book for literally everyone at every age who thinks a picture is worth a thousand words, and the words are worth like maybe fifteen words.

The goal is to make birding accessible. Knowing a creature's name is a powerful thing, and discovering the diversity in your backyard is one of the first steps to helping embrace our feathered friends (and their homes and foods) and welcoming them to our yards.

I've included 99-plus birds in this guide that are common in neighborhoods across the western USA and Canada (west of the Rocky Mountains). Not every yard is the same, of course, so if you see other types of birds that might not be in this guide, go online or go look at a more complete guide and find that bird! You'll be happy you did.

This book is a love letter to our adorable/cute/incredible/wonderful backyard birds. I hope once you start to learn about them, you don't stop there. This is just a jumping-off point. Next is joining a local birding group, planting a native plant to attract a hummingbird, learning about different ways to help increase biodiversity in our neighborhoods, and venturing out past yards and into parks on the search for more wonders of nature.

I'm so happy you picked this book up, and I can't wait for you to keep progressing on your journey! Start a list of the birds you've seen. Share your bird anecdotes with friends, don't stop talking about them at parties, send bird memes and photos to internet personalities (info@pdxbirder.com), and just enjoy the whole process that is birdwatching.

Parts of a Bird

(In this case, a Savannah Sparrow)

nape

eye line

crown stripe

lore

cheek

moustache

throat

back

breast

rump

tail

wing tip

♂ = male

♀ = female

California Quail

frilly feather

♂

black chin & face

loves
brushy cover,
hiding,
running

scalloped tummy

plump ground
forager

♀

Gambel's Quail

rusty cap

stylish plume

gray neck & back

♂

maroon-colored sides

♀

live in large coveys of 20+ birds

southwestern desert quail

9

Mourning Dove

blue eye-ring

thin bill

black dots

slender

"Coo-ooooo"

long pointy tail

widespread neighborhood & grassland dove

White-winged Dove

red eye

blue eye-ring

long face

unmarked back

White wing!

"Who cooks for you?"

attract w/ seed feeder

flocking dove of
the Southwest

Eurasian Collared-Dove

dark primaries

dark collar

short tail

pale gray overall

chunky

daytime hooter

introduced in 1970s

devours millet & grains

Band-tailed Pigeon

white &
iridescent
collar

yellow bill

lavender &
pale gray

treetop perching
forest pigeon

shallow
wing flaps
in flight

wings clap
loudly on
takeoff

Rock Pigeon
(feral)

iridescent nape

super variable plumage

Domesticated
5,000 years ago!

plump

majestic urban mascot

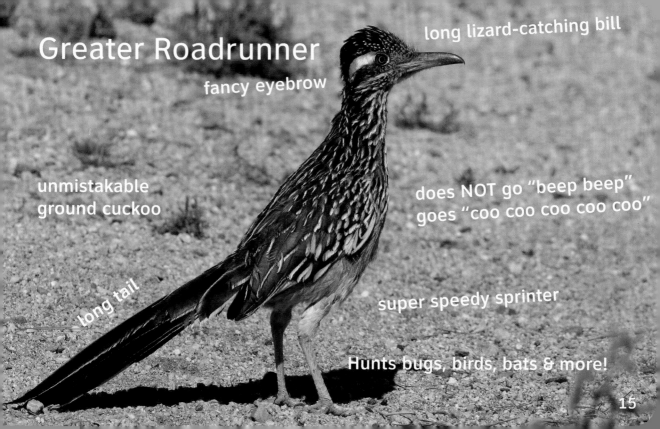

Anna's Hummingbird

♂

dark face or
irridescent
raspberry
(sunlight depending)

metalic buzz
"zuh zuh ZEEer zzeEEh"

gray-green front

plumpish

year-round western resident

16

♀/immature ♂

straight bill

dark spot

emerald
green
back

green-gray tummy

Hummingbird nectar recipe
• 1 part sugar
• 4 parts water
• no dyes
Clean often!

common neighborhood hummer

Black-chinned Hummingbird

black head

purple gorget

crisp white

in flight wings make
low pitched hum

breeds east of Cascades
in riparian habitat

18

♀/immature ♂

long bill

warm
metallic
green
back

thick wingtips ->

winters in Mexico

gray
front

pumps
tail when
hovering

Costa's Hummingbird

♂

If you live in their range, consider setting up a second hummingbird feeder so there's less competiiton between males.

pointy gorget

Purple!

green vest

kind of shy

Ocatillo-loving desert hummingbird

light eyebrow

grayish cheek

♀ /immature ♂

super clean
white front

tail & wings
same length

Desert resident:
s. CA, s. NV, s. UT & s. AZ

21

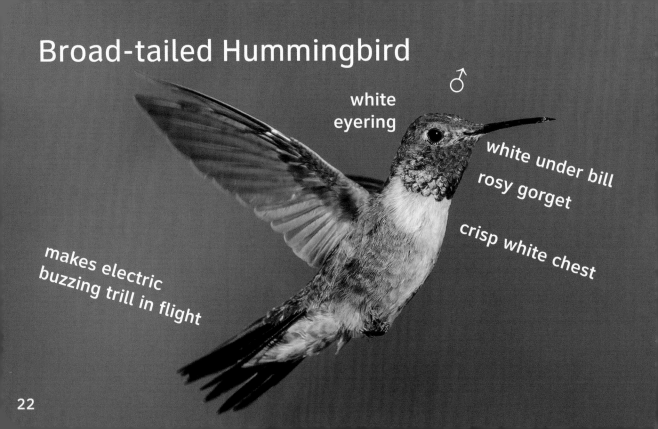

Broad-tailed Hummingbird

♂

white
eyering

white under bill

rosy gorget

crisp white chest

makes electric
buzzing trill in flight

♀/immature♂

green back
(no gold)

speckled face

buffy sides

breeds in the Intermountain West

23

Rufous Hummingbird

Firey!

♂

coppery gorget

mostly rufous back

white chest

can hear buzzy wings in flight

winters in Mexico
found from OR to AK Mar–Sep

♀/immature ♂

golden-green back

orange spot

rufous flanks

white tummy

aggressive flower defender

25

Allen's Hummingbird

green back

♂

Virtually identical to Rufous Hummingbird, but is found exclusively in Coastal California.

pointy tail feathers

orange & green

orange spot

♀

uses spider silk & moss for nests

Cooper's Hawk (adult)

dark cap

dense orange barring

stern look

light nape

steely blue back

white undertail coverts

crow-sized yard predator

head sticks out past wings

neck

(juvenile a.k.a. "juvie")

t-shape in flight

long tail

glides w/ slow, countable wingbeats

29

small,
round head

dark cap
extends
down
nape

barrel
chested

little accipiter

preys on
sparrow-sized
birds

bug-eyed

no neck

Sharp-shinned Hawk

(adult)

square tail
w/ little
to no white tip

head barely pokes out past wrists

stubby, roundish wings

(juvie)

heavily streaked chest

shorter, boxy tail

quick wingbeats in straight flight

31

Vaux's Swift

pointy wings

high-pitched
twittering chips

short tail

cigar shaped

stiff wingbeats

high flying insectivore

during fall thousands
will roost together in
chimney

Northern Flicker

black bib

mustachioed ♂

common backyard drummer

barred wings

white rump in flight

♀ lacks mustache

bill half
length
of head

♂ w/
red spot

"Pik!"

black sides & tail

2" smaller than
Hairy Woodpecker

tiny nieghborhood
woodpecker

♀ lacks
red spot

Downy Woodpecker

34

mostly found on trunks & large branches

bill same length as head

Hairy Woodpecker

mostly black back w/ speckled feathers

"Speak!"

mature forest woodpecker

35

Ladder-backed Woodpecker

red stops above eye

♂

densly barred back

desert scrub wood-pecker of the SW

streaking on chest

almost no overlaping range w/ Nuttall's

♀

36

Nuttall's Woodpecker

♀

black nape

red just on back half of head

♂

clean white outer tail feathers

spotted tummy

resident of California's oak woodlands

Red-breasted Sapsucker

red head & breast

white dot

black back

white speckling

sap-well driller & insect eater

Pileated Woodpecker

♂ w/ red mustache

♀ w/ black mustache

red crest

HUGE! (crow sized)

black body

our largest woodpecker

Olive-sided Flycatcher

peaked

chunky triangle bill

white throat

gray vest

"Quick! Three beers!"

yellow tummy

perches conspiculously

short tail

40

Western Kingbird

big gray head

gray breast

robin-sized

yellow tummy

loves an open perch

migrant tyrant flycatcher:
here Apr–Nov

41

Black Phoebe

"Fee-bee!"

"hawks" for insects

black top half

white bottom half

lots of tail bobbing

wetland flycatcher

Say's Phoebe

perching tail wagger

brown uppers

orange unders

loves fields and open spaces

nests on shelves/ mailboxes/flat spots

California Scrub-Jay

thin white eyebrow

It's not a Blue Jay!

blue head & wings

white chest blue breastband

long tail

range: w. WA–CA

Woodhouse's Scrub-Jay nearly identical but in Intermountain West

Steller's Jay

dark crest & head

Eyebrows!

bright blue wings & tail

bold & noisy

coniferous forest jay

45

American Crow

slim, straightish bill

smooth throat feathers

"Caw! Caw!"

crow sized

loves unsalted peanuts

does a lot of flapping, not much soaring

neighborhood corvid

flat-edged tail

Common Raven

soars & does acrobatics

twice the size of a crow

thick, curved bill

shaggy neck beard

"Groak! Groak!"

solitary omnivore

wedge-shaped tail

Black-billed Magpie

black

white shoulder

blue & white wings

corvid of the wild West

long tail

white tummy

Brown Creeper

Creeps!

light eyebrow

brown speckled back

white unders

"Trees, trees , beautiful trees."

flies to base of tree &
creeps up in search of
insects

49

White-breasted Nuthatch

dark crown stripe

chisel

"Mew! Mew!"

white face
& tummy

attract w/ sunflower seeds

deciduous forest
descender

Pygmy Nuthatch

plain gray uppers

small

light unders

juniper forest/high altitude nuthatch

gregarious flocking nuthatch

Bushtit

makes hanging sock-like nests from moss

hunts suet & aphids in packs

tiny bird

long tail

little bill

dark eye = ♂

light eye = ♀

when not breeding found in groups of 5–37+

Black-capped Chickadee

black cap

scraggly line between black chin & white chest

bright white in wings

attract w/ sunflower seed

"Chicka-deee-deee-deee-deee"

ubiquitous lowland chickadee

forms nucleus of many mixed flocks

Chestnut-backed Chickadee

chestnut back

squeekiest chickadee

travels in mixed
winter flocks

evergreen & oak
forest resident

55

Mountain Chickadee

white eyebrow

white cheek

cool gray back

black chin

high altitude chickadee

forms mixed flocks

Juniper & Oak Titmouse

Two species that look almost exactly the same (differntiated mostly by range). Oak Titmouse is found in CA & sw OR. Juniper Titmouse is found in the Intermountain West.

adjustable crest

adorable face

stubby bill

gray uniform

short tail

round

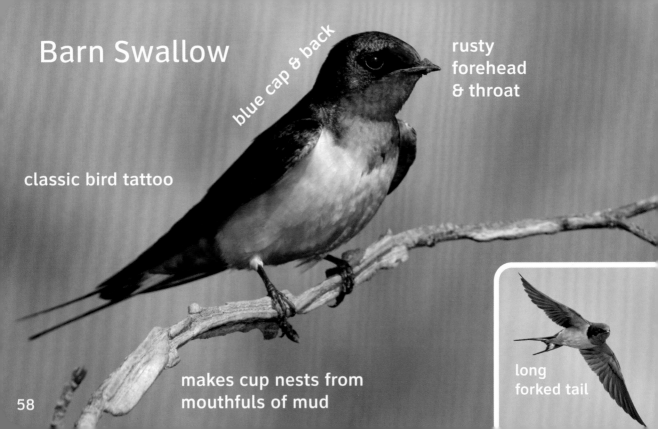

Barn Swallow

blue cap & back

rusty forehead & throat

classic bird tattoo

makes cup nests from mouthfuls of mud

long forked tail

58

Cliff Swallow

blue cap

dark back

rusty beard

buffy rump

tan headlight

colonial mud nester

Tree Swallow

metalic blue-green

dark eye-mask

white stops **below** the eye

kinda thick (for a swallow)

loves fields & wetlands

dazzling

Violet-green Swallow

green back

long wings

white on cheek goes **above** the eye

white sides on rump

quick & erratic aerialist

Bewick's Wren

barred tail

brown upperpars

thin eyebrow

light underparts

our most common yard wren

Cactus Wren

fat eyebrow

heavily patterned back

dark speckles

desert specialist wren

our beefiest wren

loves a good cactus

63

Pacific Wren

popped tail

mousy color,
mousy size,
mousy lifestyle

spots
everywhere

barred
wings
& sides

loud, complex song

lives on the forest floor

House Wren

faint eyebrow

bicolor bill

genrally brown & plain

unpopped tail

winters in the SW;
early migrant as far as BC

Ruby-crowned Kinglet

crisp yellow on black

thin bill

yellow feet

hyperactive shrub forager

pops crown when excited

Golden-crowned Kinglet

gold & black crown

dark around eyes

white eyebrow

yellowish back

mixed-flock chickadee friend

high-canopy conifer kinglet

Hutton's Vireo

big noggin

smudgy, light lores

hints of blue

thick, grayish bill

matte sheen on drab wings

methodical branch hopper

dark feet

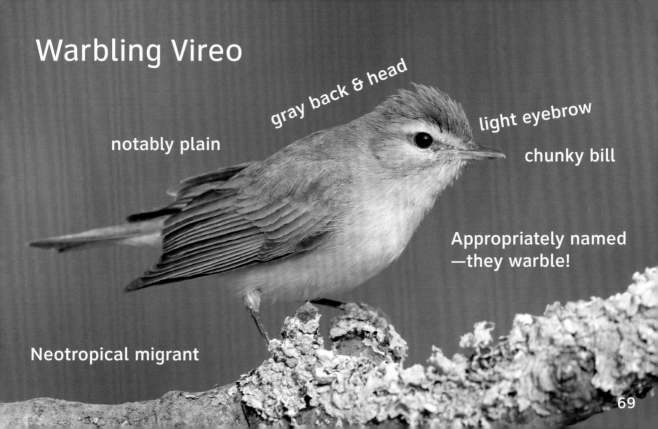

Warbling Vireo

gray back & head

notably plain

light eyebrow

chunky bill

Appropriately named —they warble!

Neotropical migrant

Cassin's Vireo

greenish gray

besepctacled

hooked bill

2 bold wingbars

yellowish armpits

joins mixed flocks of fall migrants

Western Bluebird

blue head

♂ (♀ paler)

rusty shoulders & breast

fields + trees =
bluebird habitat

blue wings

attract w/ nest boxes
& mealworms

American Robin

dark head & back

white face patterning

yellow bill

orange tummy

our most
common
thrush

Baby
bird!

Varied Thrush

pumpkin eyebrow

winter lowland visitor

pumpkin throat

breastband

spooky buzzy whistle

scalloped tummy

73

Swainson's Thrush

buffy lores & spectacles

brown back & tail w/ little contrast

"Pwip" water drop call

flutelike summer song

grayish tummy

here May–Sep

74

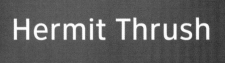

Hermit Thrush

thin white eyering

rusty wing-edge

bold spots

rusty tail

furtive forest-floor forager

winters on coast & SW
moves inland to breed

75

California Thrasher

huge curved bill

whiskery face feathers

uniformly gray

chapparal-loving mimic

exclusively lives from w. CA to Baja

Curve-billed Thrasher

yellow eye

loves to thrash
(flips over leaves
looking for insect
snacks)

white throat

round spots

found in AZ, NM & TX

Northern Mockingbird

jay-sized

territorial neighborhood mimic

dark wings & tail

loves a manmade perch (chimney, mailbox, powerline, etc.)

during breeding season even sings at night

white wing patches

Cedar Waxwing

mullet

silky browns
& yellows

waxy red wingtips

black
mask

eats berries & bugs

yellow-tipped tail

House Sparrow

gray crown

black face & throat

rufous nape & back

light gray cheek

♂

noisy

Old World sparrow of parking lots

light eyebrow

striped back

♀/immature ♂

gray-brown unders

competes w/ natives for nest boxes

81

House Finch

brightest on forehead

pale cheek

top of bill curves downward

♂

plumage ranges from red to yellow

streaked sides

bright rump

ubiquitous feeder finch

plain face & cheek

♀/immature ♂

long, blurry brown streaking

long tail

forms large, sunflower seed-eating flocks

83

Purple Finch

overall raspberry coloration

♂

red forehead & cheek

warbles from treetops in spring

clean, unstreaked look

white tummy

white eyebrow

dark cheek patch

thick triangle bill

♀/immature male

short streaks

typically found in western WA, OR, CA

85

Cassin's Finch

white eyering

cherry forehead

dark back feathers

♂

moves to lower
elevations in
fall & winter

peaked head

eyebrow

light yellowish wash

pointy triangle bill

crisp streaks

(compare to Pine Siskin page 92)

conifer-loving finch of the montane West

87

American Goldfinch

Yellow!

black forehead

orange bill

♂ breeding plumage

black wings w/ white bars

flight call: "po-ta-to-chip"

attract w/ sunflower & thistle

♂ & ♀ fully molt into sensible winter plumage

yellowish face

yellow-brown back

black wings w/ pale wingbars

unstreaked tummy

loves seedheads
& unmown yards

89

Lesser Goldfinch

black cap

greenish back

♂ breeding plumage

dull wingbars

white wing patch visible in flight

flocking thistle eaters

SW finches have black neck & back

drab greenish back

♀ /non-breeding

clean, yellowish front

our smallest finch

short tail

91

Pine Siskin

cheek & eyebrow same color

streaky back

yellow in wings & tail

pointy bill

call "rising zipper"

short notched tail

Irruptive nomadic finch: mostly found in winter but it's abundance & range are unpredictable as flocks roam in search of food.

92

Evening Grosbeak

♂

yellow brow

enormous bill

black & white wings

lemony tummy

♀

Irruptive finch: found year round
from BC to n. CA and in winters
will disperse south and east in
search of food.

93

Fox Sparrow

gray head & neck

unstreaked head

solid reddish rump

triangular tummy spots

winter hedgerow visitor

94

Song Sparrow

stripy head

gray bill

stripy back

stripy shoulders

stripy front

Stripy (& probably in your yard right now)!

95

White-crowned Sparrow

black & white crown

eye stripe

yellow-orange bill

gray cheeks

gray tummy

attract w/ seeds in a tray feeder

1st winter

Golden-crowned Sparrow

dark eyebrows

yellow forehead

1st winter plumage

dark back

light chin

large-flocking winter sparrow

fancy breeding plumage

Spotted Towhee

red eye

black head

spotted wings

white-edged tail

rufous sides

Big! (for a sparrow)

ground-scratching thicket skulker

California Towhee

sings from the shrubtops

uniformly gray

range = w. CA & s. OR

Canyon Towhee is a doppelganger, but lives in desert SW w/ no overlap.

cinnamon undertail

Chipping Sparrow

rusty cap

adult non-breeding

dark eyeline

rusty face

loves grassy woodlands & sunflower seeds

plain gray tummy

breeding plumage

baby plumage

Savannah Sparrow

fine eyeline

yellow lores

white throat

fine streaking

white tummy

grassland songbird

Dark-eyed Junco

Oregon form

dark head & dark eyes

pink bill

brownish sides & back

white outer tail feathers

light tummy

joins large winter sparrow flocks

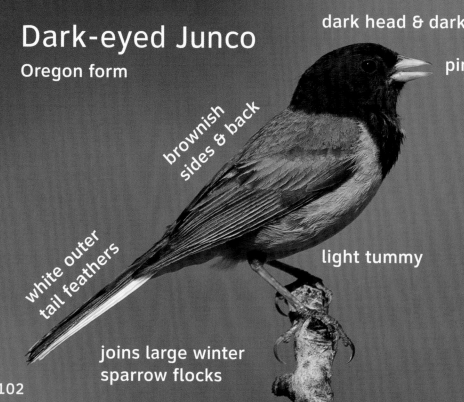

Slate-colored form

Pink-sided form

Lark Sparrow

harlequin mask

WOW! stunning dream sparrow

black dot

clean white unders

found in grassy habitats w/ sparse shrubs

Bullock's Oriole

chunky wingbar

eyeline

♂

attracted
to jelly
feeders

black throat

found in deciduous
trees, loves cottonwoods

slight eyeline

pointy bill

white wingbars

♀/immature

mostly gray unders

Neotropical migrant

weave intricate hanging nests

105

Hooded Oriole

clean orange hood

♂

black throat & face

double wingbar

long tail

seeks out palm trees

106

range = CA, AZ, s. TX

♀/immature

brownish back

downcurved bill

mostly orange unders

attract w/ jelly, oranges, hummingbird feeders

Red-winged Blackbird

red & yellow shoulder patch

downcurved bill

loud distinct song
"Jus-Tin Beee-Ber"

♂

black body

loves sunflowers
& bird feeders

light eyebrow

pointy bill

found near wetlands

♀ (that's right)

rufous edged feathers

dense streaking

often feeds w/ sparrow flocks but its the big one of the group

winner of the most misidentified bird award

109

Brown-headed Cowbird

matte brown head

big cone bill

♂

iridescent
black body

chunky

joins large mixed
blackbird flocks

short tail

110

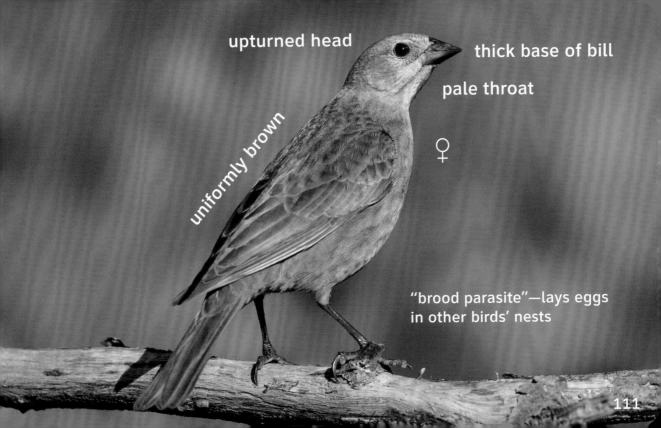

upturned head

thick base of bill

pale throat

uniformly brown

♀

"brood parasite"—lays eggs in other birds' nests

111

Brewer's Blackbird

light eye

purplish head

♂

glossy back

greenish body

our native parking lot bird

dark eye

♀ /immature

medium pointy bill

average seeming proportions

dark wings

brown body

medium long tail

hunts for seeds in large packs

113

Great-tailed Grackle

♂

light eye

iridescent
purple & blue

BIG!

large social
blackbirds

really great tail

long legs

114

flat head

light eye

♀/immature

long down-curved bill

twice as large as Brewer's Blackbird

Southwest resident

115

Yellow-headed Blackbird

(appropriately named)

shockingly loud screaming call

white wing patch

found near wetlands but love seed feeders

♀

Yellow-rumped Warbler
(Audubon's subspecies)

♀

"Chep!"

yellow throat

streaky tummy

our year-round warbler (eats berries & suet in winter)

♂ breeding

yellow armpits

(Myrtle subspecies)

light eyebrow

♀

white throat

all with yellow rumps

often heard chipping & seen flycatching

♂ breeding

black mask

119

Orange-crowned Warbler

subtle orange

broken eyering

pointy
bill

year-round
coastal warbler

drab
greenish

Some populations
winter in TX, AZ, CA &
breed in thick conifer
forests of the West.

Townsend's Warbler

stunning
face pattern

♂

black
chin

yellow breast

conifer-loving
winter warbler

♀

streaky

Yellow Warbler

black & yellow wings ♂

Bright yellow!

stout bill

rusty streaking

found in cottonwoods
& willows in moist spots

♀

Wilson's Warbler

black toupée

olive back

♂

yellow face & front

unstreaked

♀

found low in dense brush & thickets

Common Yellowthroat

black mask

♂

Yellow throat!

"witchity witchity witchity"

yellow undertail

really are pretty "common" near marshes, wetlands, & brushy fields

brown back & face

gray cheek

yellow undertail

forages low & hides in tall grass

♀

Western Tanager

fiery feathers

black back

two wingbars

frog-like "pridit" call

yellow undertail

hunts insects in spring/summer, berries in fall/winter

gets red pigmentation from eating bugs

♀ /immature

yellowish head & chest

grayish back

chunky bill

larger than warbler smaller than a robin

often found at top of conifers

127

Black-headed Grosbeak

black head

♂

enormous bill

b&w wings

2 wing bars

orange chest

Neotropical migrant

sounds like a melodic robin

Lazuli Bunting

♂

Turquoise!

chunky white wingbars

rusty orange

late-spring migrant

peaked head

finch-like bill

♀ /immature

unstreaked
orangish
chest

light wingbars

loves fieldside
brambles

131

DEDICATION

To my daughter Margo and all future birdwatchers,
may this book inspire a lifelong love for birds, while
reminding us to do our best to conserve their
habitats for the enjoyment of all.

SEYMORE GULLS, a.k.a. Eric Carlson, is a Portland, Oregon based bird enthusiast. He creates books and videos to educate his audience and inspire a love of birds. Seymore also leads weekly beginner bird walks where he shares his binoculars and knowledge with all who attend. He believes that birding can change the world and it's his personal mission to get as many people as possible to start taking notice of the wonderful creatures around them.

BRIAN E. SMALL is a full-time professional bird and nature photographer. For more than 30 years, he has traveled widely across North America to capture images of birds in their native habitats. He served as the photo editor for *Birding* magazine for 15 years. Small grew up in Los Angeles, graduated from U.C.L.A. in 1982, and still lives there today with his wife Ana, daughter Nicole, and son Tyler.

SPECIES INDEX

Goodbye
and good
birding!